ESSENTIAL FLY PATTERNS FOR LAKES AND STREAMS

Caitlin Press Inc.
8100 Alderwood Road, Halfmoon Bay, BC V0N 1Y1
www.caitlin-press.com

Text and cover design by Vici Johnstone
Cover image from Unsplash
Printed in Canada

Caitlin Press Inc. acknowledges financial support from the Government of Canada and the Canada Council for the Arts, and the Province of British Columbia through the British Columbia Arts Council and the Book Publisher's Tax Credit.

| Canada Council for the Arts Conseil des Arts du Canada | BRITISH COLUMBIA ARTS COUNCIL | Funded by the Government of Canada | Canada |

Library and Archives Canada Cataloguing in Publication

Essential fly patterns for lakes and streams : tips for tying your own flies / Brian Smith.

Names: Smith, Brian (Brian Ivan), 1947- author.

Identifiers: Canadiana 2019005025X | ISBN 9781773860008 (softcover)

Subjects: LCSH: Fly tying—Handbooks, manuals, etc.

Classification: LCC SH451 .S65 2019 | DDC 688.7/9124—dc23

ESSENTIAL FLY PATTERNS FOR LAKES AND STREAMS

Tips for Tying Your Own Flies

BRIAN SMITH

CAITLIN PRESS

Dragon Lake, Quesnel, BC. Photo Brian Smith

To my wife, Lois, who unselfishly encourages me to pursue this passion of fly-fishing and patiently spends countless hours waiting for me to come home from my journeys afield: thank you for your love and caring.

To my fellow members of the Polar Coachman Fly Fishers, and especially Erich Franz, whose fine camera work produced all of the flies' photos for this book; thank you from the bottom of my heart for your assistance, and for your encouragement to write another.

Stellako River. "Nice trout!" Photo Brian Smith

Graham Smith "hugging" a Stellako River rainbow. Photo Brian Smith

CONTENTS

Author and daughter, BJ Smith, fishing on Stellako River, BC.
Photo Lois Smith

BJ Smith and rainbow trout, Crooked River, BC. Photo Brian Smith

INTRODUCTION

This book, which chronicles the fly-tying journey of my life, is the accumulation of fifty years of fly-fishing thoughts, discussions, book reading and noble experiments. Many of my trials at the vise have been disastrous and poor-looking models, but out of the mess and research has come wisdom that resulted in more and better prototypes. This has led me to the sombre realization that the perfect creation of an insect replica at the vise does not or will not exist. The best we can possibly do, in the immortal words of my late friend and mentor, Jack Shaw, is "giving it our best shot to create impressions of flies that will catch fish and depict correctly four basic principles of a good trout fly: size, shape, colour and attitude (movement)." You will notice most of these principles in all my fly patterns.

The *size* and *shape* of your impression is most important. Trout feed selectively much of the time, binge-feeding only when conditions are ripe for it. If, for example, fish are gorging on chironomid pupae that are staging on the bottom of the lake, they will be circling through their larder with mouths open, eating everything that looks like a pupa. As long as your impression is close in both size and shape, it will be victimized as trout food.

Another consideration is *colour and appearance.* Using the same example of a chironomid pupa that is staging to begin its pupation ascent to the surface, it is important to mimic the bubble of air gas that forms under the pupa's exoskeleton. Combined with the colour and likeness of the hatch in progress, this is achieved with the use of beads, tinsel flash and clear coat on your models, exuding the impression of translucence and the "I'm ready to hatch" attitude. Also consider why sparkle dubbings are such effective body materials—they capture light and emit a lifelike personality to your flies. I use them extensively in my patterns.

The suggestion or action of *movement* is often the clincher in the deal. The use of a head bead commonly used on chironomid pupae is two-fold: if you work the fly with very short, inch-long strips and pauses, it will mimic the bobbing action of an anxious chironomid pupa getting ready to ascend; secondly, the bead adds weight to the hook so it reaches the feeding zone faster. Unlike most fly tyers, I like to add a small throat hackle and a twist of herl to my pupae, again creating the illusion of movement and adding to the overall impression of the insect's thorax and wings that I am trying to create.

You will recognize many of the patterns in this book—not much is new in the way a bug looks. It is not a book on bug entomology. I have, however, tweaked a lot of the patterns I have seen and tied over the years, and this chronicle is an accumulation of what I have observed, doing it "my way" to achieve what I think is a better result—productive and better-looking flies!

I confess to being a trout bum, the last several years preferably with a dry fly. I have never fished for or caught bass, pike, pickerel, perch, Muskie or the like—all the species of trout and salmon have been my game. A lot of water has passed under the bridges in my over seventy years of life. The pursuit of trout with a fly has taken up over fifty of them, and I have come to realize that there is much water that will never see my flies, but I have no regrets or sorrow about that—water is water, whether it is "home" water or new water, and all fishing is good fishing. I'm happy to have found it... enjoy!

Author fishing the evening hatch under the Glenannan Bridge, Stellako River, BC. Photo Colin Ewart

Instructions for Tying My Fly Patterns

Fly-tying Tips for the Rest of Your Life

I've been tying flies for almost fifty years and have bungled and thought my way through most fly-tying operations. Some of these tips come from instruction books, but most are "light bulb" thoughts I've worked out myself. After repeating these tips a few times, they will become part of your fly-tying soul too.

In the pattern recipes, these fly-tying tips are numbered in brackets (< >), instructing the tyer which tip(s) I use to tie the pattern.

I like fine wire hooks for most of my dry fly ties, especially hook sizes #6 to 14—they float hackles and bodies better than standard heavy wire hooks. They are, however, susceptible to bending, so you cannot "horse" your fish with them. Fine wire hooks are ideal for the split cane, whippy rods I like to use for small river fishing, where casts are short and finesse is important. I've lost too many fine trout on fine wire hooks in small sizes #14–22, and prefer straight eye, standard wire hooks like the Tiemco 101 so I can see the eye and knot them better with my aging eyes. It's your choice.

Hooks for wet fly nymph fishing need to reflect the insects' body lengths and curvatures. For larvae, nymphs, pupae and emerger imitations, I try to capture these characteristics with various standard wire hook lengths from 1X to 5X long, adding curvature where I see it fits. For example, I tie a darner dragonfly nymph on a Mustad R75 hook, which is a 5X length, but will tie the red-shouldered dragonfly nymph on a Mustad R73, which is a 3X length, because this insect is shorter and has a squat appearance. Pupae patterns are well suited to curved hooks in various lengths like the Tiemco 2457 or 200R, or the Mustad C49/67 or C53S, since they simulate a bent, wiggling body motion better than a straight hook does. For emergers, I like curved hooks but fine wire, since I want them to float; the Tiemco 2487 and the Mustad C49 suit this purpose.

I prefer tying threads that will lie flat on the hook shank rather than round. UTC thread by Wapsi is my first choice: 70 denier thread for hooks sizes #10 and smaller and 140 denier for hooks sizes #8 and larger. Unless you are spinning deer hair directly onto the hook shank (for example, on a Goddard Caddis), always apply a base layer of thread onto the shank. This provides an anchor for all of the materials applied.

1.   Apply all the materials in the order listed in my tying instructions—they will come up the shank and finish in a better fashion.

2.   Learn to tie with your scissors in hand—you'll never lose them on the bench and will save yourself many pick-up steps.

3.   Use bobbins to hold ribbing wire, lead-free wire, chenille, embroidery thread, floss, tinsel, etc.—almost anything that comes on a spool or card that can be threaded through a bobbin. Buy half a dozen inexpensive bobbins for this purpose and switch them out when needed, keeping your most popular materials on a bobbin at all times. I save and use empty tying thread spools to load my carded fly-tying materials.

4.   To attach ribbing, floss, etc. that will be wound up or down the shank, use a bobbin. Attach material on the shank one eye-length behind the hook eye, and wrap and bind it with tying thread all the way to the rear of the shank. If ribbing with wire, do a half-wrap at the rear and secure with thread behind and front—your ribs will never slip out or slide off the end of your fly body again, and the ribbing will start perfectly every time.

5.   To wrap lead-free wire underbodies, use a bobbin. Attach on top of the shank. Affix with tying thread along the top of the shank with light pressure to the desired end point of the lead underbody; return thread to the starting point, wrap lead wire back to front and tie off. When wrapping underbodies, always leave at least a hook-eye gap at each terminal to begin and finish the rest of the fly.

6.   To attach feather hackles to the shank, discard feather butt waste, trim the hackle butt to 5 mm in length on both sides with scissors, attach with 3 thread wraps and give a little tug to separate the feather barbs from the shank—this will eliminate errant barbs. For wet flies, attach

the glossy side of the feather to the front; for dry flies, do the reverse and attach the flat side to the front of the hook. Also see tip 17.

7.   For shellbacks on scuds (apply Midge Flex as the last step), after palmering hackle, trim the hackle fibres flat over the body, then trim each side of the Midge Flex tip to achieve a picket fence appearance. Tie it in at the head, lay it over the body (tight, but don't stretch it), apply the ribbing material in 6–8 turns to the head and tie off the fly. Trim the appendage to a V-shape with a scissor-cut at a 30° slant—it should protrude downwards off the hook curve.

8.   To attach throat, collar, thorax and overwing feathers, choose an appropriate *whole* feather for the size of the hook. Discard feather plume waste, preen the remaining barbules backwards to expose the stem, and clip out the tip of the feather (should now have a V). Attach by the stem to the shank with 3 firm wraps. Give a little tug on the stem to position the barbs at the correct length and tie off—perfect every time!

9.   For marabou and feather tails/shucks, use the same cleaning, clipping and application procedures as in tip 8, but the tail is applied at the end of the shank. For an upright split tail, take a turn of thread under the tail fibres at the end of the shank, which "lifts" the tail upward to the ideal position and separates the fibres.

10.   For ostrich or peacock collars and chenille bodies, use the same procedures outlined in tip 6 to expose the base, but strip the butt with your thumb and forefinger instead of scissors.

11.   To apply bead heads, I use a dab of dubbing wax on my thumb and middle finger to pick up the bead. Crimp the hook barb, slip the bead onto the hook shank above the vise jaws, build up thread behind the eye until the bead fits tightly, apply a drop of head cement to the thread, slide the bead over, and tie off the fly in front of the bead. Reattach thread behind the bead. Build up a thread base behind the bead, but leave an eye-length gap and cavity for body materials to enter. For chironomid patterns using beads, use the same method, but reverse the bead on the shank, larger hole to hook eye, tie in the white gill filament first and then slip the bead over it.

12. A deer hide has many colours, lengths and various textures of hair from fine to coarse. When working with deer hair, depending on the size of fly I am tying, I vary these characteristics to suit the pattern: a short length and fine texture for flies sizes #14–22; a medium length and medium texture for sizes #10–12; and long length and coarse texture for sizes #6-8. Use less hair rather than more for your flies: about 2-mm width for sizes #18–22; 3 mm for #14–16; 4 mm for #10–12; 5 mm for the balance of sizes. Cut and clean a stack of hair with your fingers and a "nit" comb, and trim the butt ends square. Use a hair stacker to achieve consistent lengths: insert the stack into the hair stacker tips first, hold the stacker at a 45° angle and tap the device on your open palm. Use 140 denier threads for tying flies that require "stacking" and "spinning."

13. For dry fly hackles, choose a saddle or neck hackle 1.5 times the gap of your hook size, or use a hackle gauge to measure the hackles. Use tip 6 for cleaning and trimming. On the hook shank, leave 2 eye-lengths behind the eye for the hackle and head—3 eye-lengths if the pattern includes a wing. Install dry fly hackles with the flat side to the eye, and apply a small drop of Super Glue to the tie-in point (it helps stiffen the barbs). For hackling around upright wings, the rule is 2 turns of the hackle behind the wing and 4 turns in front. Trim the centre barbules only on the bottom of the dry-fly hackle fibres to an inverted V by clipping the middle barbs, which helps eliminate leader twist and allows your fly to ride the water correctly, with support from the outer barbules. After tying, I spray all my dry flies that I wish to float high (except emergers) with clear silicone boot spray.

14. I like to use body or wing feathers from grouse or cock pheasant throat neck feathers for my nymph swimming "legs." Use a whole feather with the correct length of fibres for your fly, discard waste, preen enough remaining barbs for legs and to expose the stem. Tie in the feather upside down at the stem point, with the tip pointing towards the hook's eye, to the top of the shank in front of the wing-case with 3 firm wraps; give a little tug to separate the feather from the shank and thorax. Apply the thorax in front of the legs feather, lay the feather over the thorax and tie it in; finish with the wing-case over the thorax and legs.

15. For deer hair wings for mayflies, choose and prepare as described in tip 12. Measure to the body length of the shank, tie in with the tips pointing to the rear and bind tightly in front of the wings with 10 very tight wraps, so the hairs won't spin on the shank. Lift the wing straight up, apply a thread block of 10 wraps *behind* the wing, and make 4–5 wraps of thread *through* the wing. Apply a dab of head cement to the wing base to stiffen the wing.

16. To tie mayfly extended abdomens, begin 2 eye-lengths behind the eye. Tie in Mayfly Tails or moose hairs parallel and on top of the hook shank, extended past the rear slightly longer than body-length. Attach 6–8 deer hairs for the abdomen 2 eye-lengths from the hook eye, which should extend slightly shorter than the tail's full length, and spiral thread to the hook bend in 5–6 wraps. Reverse the hook in the vise, hold the deer hairs tightly and continue to wrap up the tails in 4–5 wraps, then wrap back to the hook bend. Reverse the hook to its original position and continue to wrap thread back to the tie-in point. Trim the ends of the deer hair abdomen to a short stub, leaving Mayfly Tails or moose hairs projecting upwards. If desired for strength, apply a coat of Sally Hansen's to the abdomen and let it dry before proceeding.

17. For palmered hackle, if using saddle hackle (my preference for small flies), tie in by the hackle's butt; if using cock capes (leeches, buggers), tie in by the tip. For capes, discard the feather waste at the butt, preen the barbs at the tip to expose the stem, apply to the shank at the stem point, and give a little tug to separate the feather from the fly body. If required on some flies (caddisfly larva), trim both sides of the hackle to the hook gape before palmering. For flies with overwing(s) or shellbacks, trim the palmered fibres flat to the top of the body after applying the hackle.

18. To stack or apply deer or elk hair wings (Caddisfly Traveller Adult), use UTC 140 denier thread and use only "select" coarse deer or elk hairs. Refer to tip 12 for cleaning and stacking; use 5 mm-width stacks. After stacking, squeeze and separate the hairs by rolling them in your thumb and forefinger, and then apply them flat on edge (as opposed to round), which will stand the hairs up nicely. For the correct length of the stacks, measure them only to the length of the previous stack, and when applying them to the shank, grip and hold the stack tightly on top of the hook shank, make your first 2 turns of thread just firmly enough to hold the hairs in place, and the next 3–4 turns very tightly to prevent the stack from spinning on the hook, and then loosen your grip on the hair stack. As you affix the deer hairs, advance the tying thread *along* the hook as opposed to binding in one spot; this helps prevent the stack from splaying.

19. To prepare down-wing wings for caddisflies/stoneflies/hoppers, spray the entire primary feather of pheasant, goose, duck or turkey with workable fixative from an art supply store, which will stiffen the barbs but leave them pliable. Fold the feather strip in half lengthwise, apply to the shank and cut to length with scissors held at 30° angle.

20. To set antennae on dry flies (sedges, stoneflies), use stripped feather hackle, stiff boar bristle hairs or marabou plume, which comes in many dyed colours. Pluck the hair or plume with thumb and forefinger to curl the antennae *before* you tie it in, which flattens the stem and eliminates twisting. I tie these dry flies with antennae for display or shadow boxes, but usually eliminate them for flies that I fish with.

21. For hackle tips for tails (damselfly), the first step is to use a body material of dubbing tied at the end of the hook shank in a tail ball, which will separate the tails. Choose hackles, clean waste, and strip the barbs to the desired tail length. Install at the stem with 3 snug wraps; give a little tug to each feather to correct its length.

22. For ostrich or peacock herls and marabou fibres in a dubbing loop, choose materials, trim them to even lengths, and tie them in by their tips. Make 5–6 twists of material around the tying thread loop, install the dubbing twist tool and counter-twist 10–12 turns to form a dubbed rope of materials.

23. For Larva Lace or V-rib "eyes," first build a small dam of tying thread at the hook eye (so the eyes don't slip forward). Choose a 10-mm piece of Larva Lace or V-rib, and burn one end. Install it on top of the hook shank behind the dam with cross-wraps, with the burnt end in correct position; trim and burn the other end to an equal length.

24. For bead heads for balanced leeches, use a jig hook, insert the bead onto a ½-inch finishing nail with the large eye of the bead to the front, where it will jam on the nail head. Wrap the nail to the top of the hook shank.

25. Make your own Velcro comb. To fluff or even dubbed bodies and leech yarn, the tool I use is an ice cream stick with a strip of Velcro glued to the tip with Super Glue. The sticks come in various sizes.

26. To use glass beads as eyes, buy them at a dollar store. I cut 20 lb. mono line to a 7 mm length, burn one end of the mono line, insert both beads, and then burn the other end to the length desired. Touch up with a black Sharpie marker. I like to complete the head with herls before I touch the thorax procedure. Use tip 23 to install and tip 22 for herls.

27. Embroidery thread for underbodies lies flat, and comes in a multitude of colours. Use with a bobbin—less waste, better control.

28. For foam wing-cases or bodies, buy sheet foam at Walmart (this comes with many colours to a pack), cut into desired strips with an X-acto knife. For two-coloured hoppers, cement 2 strips together with Super Glue.

29. Make Legs-on-a-Stick with knotted pheasant tail sword fibres— buy them called this, or knot your own.

30. Spun deer hair and bullet heads: leave 3-4 eye-lengths worth of space for the head. Use tips 12 and 18 for cleaning and preparing. Using 5 mm bunches, apply short wing and throat by laying hairs tips rearwards with 2 loose wraps, then very tight wraps, allowing the hair to spin. Block the front of each section with several tight wraps of thread. Continue up the shank with 5-mm bunches (tips trimmed) cross-wrapping with thread, letting them spin and packing them tightly against each other with your thumb and forefinger or a packing tool. Trim the head: for hoppers—flat on bottom, square on sides and top; for bullet heads, use curved scissors and begin at the hook's eye—flat on bottom, sloping to the rear on the top and sides. To finish trimming, remove the hook from the vise and work from the rear of the head. Takes a little practice....

31. You can purchase tape-on eyes, but I prefer to paint mine on. Purchase bottles of Crafter's Acrylic paint in black, yellow, silver, gold and white from a dollar store. Allow 2–3 eye-lengths to complete the head. Use UTC 140 denier white thread for tying the fly and build a good head; after concluding, squeeze the head flat on both sides with non-serrated pliers. Apply a coat of Sally Hansen's nail polish; allow to dry. Using the head of a finishing nail put a dab of the desired eye colour on each side of the head and allow it to dry. With a smaller nail head or a toothpick, apply a dab of the desired pupil colour. After drying, apply 2 coats of Sally Hansen's or UV cement.

32. To attach Booby Eyes, place a tying thread at the mid-point of the material, make 3–4 turns around the foam, transfer it to the hook and continue to wind the thread until the foam is lodged in place.

33. To attach "flash" over bodies and Antron "spent" wings on mayflies made with materials like Flashabou or Krystal Flash, take 2 or 3 strands, fold them once in half, transfer them onto the bobbin thread at the fold, bring the thread tight and tie it to the top of the shank, laying them to the rear. Trim to length. This method also works well for Antron fibres on spent wings, Glo Yarn on egg flies, etc.

34. For midge or chironomid gills in front of bead heads, see tip 11. Use a fine Antron-like white Glo Yarn or Midge Gills on a bobbin, one you can split for smaller portions.

35. For upright hackle tip wings, choose 2 hackle tips of same size and colour; preen waste on both sides to expose the short tips of the feathers. Measure to the body length of the fly, and lay both on top of the shank tips forward 3 eye-lengths behind the eye, secure with 3–4 tight wraps of thread. Lift and block the tips in front with thread, separate tips and cross-wrap to desired angles of 30°.

36. To use moose, deer, calf, etc., hair tails for dry flies, choose, clean and stack as described in tip 12. Tie in 2–3 eye-lengths behind the eye and wrap down the shank to the hook bend, then take 2 wraps under to lift and split the hairs.

37. The key to tying dubbed bodies or thoraxes is to use minimal materials: the "less is more" principle. Use dubbing wax on your thumb and forefinger. Apply dubbing sparingly to a 10-cm length of waxed tying thread, insert a dubbing twister hook, pull the bobbin thread back to the shank, spin tool counter-clockwise about 12–15 turns to form a loop rope; apply to the shank and afterwards use a Velcro comb to smooth the body.

38. To "post" a wing on dry fly parachute hackles, install the wing as described in tip 15, but don't wrap through the wing. Prepare it for posting by blocking the wing upright front and rear. Take all the wing fibres in one hand, and with your other hand, make 5–6 turns of thread up and down the wing's upright butt, making a place for the parachute hackle to sit. Install the hackle behind the wing, flat side down, finish the thorax, and then wrap the hackle up and down the post for 5–6 turns. Tie the hackle off *on the post*, cement and finish the fly.

39. Before attaching biots or tails on nymphs (stonefly or mayfly), build a small dubbing ball of body material at the hook bend, which will keep the biots or tail fibres separated on the shank. Apply biots to each side of the dubbing ball; apply tail fibres on top of the ball.

40. CDC (Cul de Canard) are the duck's oil gland feathers and are used for feather wings, underwings, and trailing shucks. Use the entire feather—clean and discard waste, lay the exposed stem on top of the hook shank, apply 3 light turns of thread, and give a light tug to set the feather at the desired length on the shank. I use a lot of these on my caddisfly and stonefly dry flies for creeks and rivers: they help float the wings better, giving width and a lifelike attitude to the fly.

41. For deer hair wing-cases (midge or chironomid adults) and emergers, treat the tail and wing-case with separate bunches of deer hair. For a wing-case, choose and clean as described in tip 12, clip tips, install directly in front of the tail butt, install the body and then pull the wing-case over the body. For emergers, I use two methods (see mayfly emerger photos): 1) tie the wing-case hair by the butts before and behind the thorax and wrap the case over the thorax; or 2) tie the wing-case by the butts facing the rear in front of the thorax and trim to thorax length, tips up.

42. For streamer trailing hooks on wire, use an articulated shank. Place the hook in the vise with the open clip upwards, tie in thread, close the clip with a double wrap and take the tying thread to the shank eye. Cut a 10-cm length of Rio 20 lb Wire Bite, and string both free ends through the eye of the articulated shank, leaving a 4-cm loop of wire behind the articulated shank. Double the free ends back under the shank and catch all four strands of wire with the tying thread. Bind wire down and back up the shank with a double wrap of thread. The hook is installed after the fly is tied (hook point up) by compressing the wire loop and running it through the trailing hook's eye. Finally, pull the loop to the rear, bring it over the hook point, and then draw the wire loop forward against the eye.

43. For Mylar or tinsel body minnows and streamers, counter-wrap with a wire rib for added strength. If you use a bobbin, the tinsel will twist, and you will need to untwist it as you proceed. If the pattern has a tail, tie the rib and tail first, starting one eye-length behind the eye, wrapping all the way down and back to the tie-in point. Clip the tinsel to a point, tie it in and wrap the tinsel all the way down and back using both hands, overlapping on the return wraps, then counter-wrap with wire. Coat with Sally Hansen's or flexible cement.

44. For egg flies, use 140 denier tying thread and a heavy hook, and you won't need to add weight to your fly. Cut 2–3 strands of Glo Yarn in about 2-cm lengths. Spread the strand, and in the middle of each, attach securely on top of the hook; with your fingers, spin the yarn around the hook top and bottom and tie off. Add additional strands and stack them until the hook is full. On top of the hook, take all the stacked strands and pull straight up, and then trim tightly with scissors; repeat on the bottom of the hook. For the veil, attach a 5-mm width behind the eye in front of the hook with 2 wraps, spread the veil around the eye, finish the head and tie off; trim to egg length.

45. Primary feather barbs for nymphs' and dry flies' abdomens (mayflies, emergers) are typically cock pheasant sword or natural and dyed goose quills. Use 1–3 barbs depending on the size of the fly. Pluck them from the stem and trim the tips. With goose barbs, you will notice a cuticle that projects from the butt; apply with the tips up for a rough textured body (nymphs), and with tips down for a smooth body (dry flies). For nymphs, counter-wind with wire for added strength; for dry flies, apply a coat of Sally Hansen's.

46. Belly or overwing hairs of calf, bucktail, deer, etc., on streamers and minnows use 140 denier thread. Clean, stack and trim the hairs to even lengths as described in tip 12. Measure hairs 1.5 times longer than the hook's shank lengths; take 2 turns of thread around the hairs and transfer to the bottom of the hook, pull the hairs to the correct length, secure with more thread wraps and continue with the rest of the fly. For overwings, use the same procedures on top of the shank.

A fly in the vice—Salmonfly, Down-wing Adult. Photo Brian Smith

ESSENTIAL TROUT FLIES FOR STILL WATER

Freshwater Shrimp (Scud)

Many fly-tyers tie scuds on curved hooks such as a Tiemco 2457 or a Mustad C49S; I don't. The only time scuds are in curved fetal positions is when they are resting or frightened. I will tie a few on curved hooks to imitate that mood; however, shrimp travel by swimming in a straight body position, so you should tie a bunch on straight-shanked hooks like the Tiemco 100 or the Mustad R50 models.

Scuds dine on lake vegetation and decaying organic matter, and their body colours reflect what they eat. Typical shrimp colours in the Thompson-Cariboo regions are pale olive, chartreuse, Naples yellow and even an opalescent bluish-pink in many waters. In northern BC, you typically see freshwater shrimp in dark olive, brown olive, and a sandy tan tone in clear water lakes such as Wicheeda. I use sparkle dubbings to impart the "wet look" of scuds, and a pregnant imitation is often deadly—tie it the same as Gammarus, but add a turn of egg-orange chenille in the middle of the body.

There are two scuds that you should imitate: Gammarus and Hyalella. They are both tied in the same manner, except the Hyalella is small and paler in colour, and is tied on hook sizes #14–18.

Gammarus Shrimp

Hook: Tiemco 100 #8–12
Thread: UTC 70, olive
Ribs: fine gold wire; 6–8 turns over the shellback <3, 4>
Hackle: medium olive, one side stripped; palmer 5–6 turns over the body and trim flat on top <17>
Underbody: .020 mm lead wire; 8–10 turns in the middle of the hook shank <5>
Body: Stillwater Solutions Sparkle Blend dubbing, olive <37>
Shellback: 5 mm Midge Flex over the body; trimmed at the rear to form a tail appendage <7>

left: Gammarus Shrimp; right: pregnant Gammarus Shrimp

Hyalella Shrimp

Hook: Tiemco 100 #14–18

Thread: UTC 70, grey brown

Ribs: fine gold wire; 5–6 turns over the shellback <3, 4>

Hackle: none—picked-out body dubbing simulates legs

Underbody: .015 mm lead wire; 6–8 wraps around the middle of the shank <5>

Body: dubbing, Ligas 42, grey olive <37>

Shellback: 5 mm Midge Flex, clear, over body; trimmed at the rear to form an appendage <7>

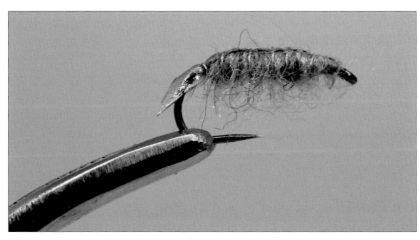

Hyalella Shrimp

Leeches

No fly box is complete without a solid assortment of leech patterns. I have come full circle with my leech imitations, and must confess to having far too many for the 7 per cent of a trout's diet that they fill. Leeches are a favourite searching pattern for many fly fishers, and rightly so. I've caught a lot of trout on leeches over the last fifty years, and they are "big fish" flies, a pattern that will often save an otherwise uneventful fishing day.

Leeches are found in all lakes and slow-moving streams around the world. Common colours are mottled combinations of olive, brown, maroon, grey and almost black. In my experience, fish favour the young of the year over large, 8- to 10-cm long, mature leeches—a #6 hook should be the maximum size for leech imitations, and #14s tied on long-shank hooks are often wildly successful, especially during late summer and the autumn.

During the 1970s and '80s, I tied and fished Jack Shaw's blood leech pattern most of the time: a #8 long-shank hook, a maroon mohair body, 2 bunches of brown-purple pheasant flank tied at the midpoint and the head. I developed my own successful pattern I called the Blood Bugger in the 1990s: a #8–14 long-shank hook, a black marabou tail and a maroon-purple dubbed body with black, palmered hackle. Both of these are still fine producers, but lately I've gone to a rabbit strip leech that I tie on an up-eye steelhead/salmon hook, Mustad SL73 #6–10. The fly has incredible undulating movement in the water, just like a leech.

Another popular leech pattern is the Micro Leech in sizes #14–16, but I honestly believe trout eat this as a chironomid rather than as a leech. A fly box is incomplete without what is called a Balanced Leech, tied on a jig hook to ride upside down over productive shoal water using an indicator system, much like chironomid fishing—let it hang there and give it the odd little twitch to suggest movement.

Rabbit Strip Leech

Hook: Mustad SL73 #6–10
Thread: UTC 70, black
Underbody: .020 mm lead wire; 10–12 turns at the front portion of the shank <5>

Tail: rabbit zonker strip, black

Body: dubbing, Metz Arizona Simi-seal, colour bloody leech; comb before the wing application <37>

Wing: rabbit zonker strip, black; hair length to equal tail portion

Comment: Alternative wing/body colours are olive zonker/Stillwater Sparkle dubbing, olive; brown zonker/Stillwater Sparkle dubbing, brown; or black zonker/Stillwater Sparkle dubbing, black. Try not to put too much rabbit on the hook because you will stifle the fly's action in the water. I split my zonker strips to about 3-mm width; trim the skin to a picket fence point and tie it in, then trim the skin to point again at the free section.

Rabbit Strip Blood Leech

Rabbit Strip Leech Olive

Micro Leech

Hook: Tiemco 100 #14–18
Thread: UTC 70, black
Bead: gold 3/32 <11>
Tail: black marabou <9>
Ribs: fine red wire <3, 4>
Body: black marabou strands spun in a dubbing loop <22>
Collar: black ostrich herl; 2–3 turns <10>

Comment: Alternative colours for bead heads, ribs, tails and bodies are copper/copper/maroon or brown; black/silver/black; or gold/gold/olive.

Micro Leech

Balanced Leech

Hook: Mustad jig 32833 #6–10 or Partridge 60° jig hook #10–14
Thread: UTC 70, black
Bead head: 1/8 tungsten bead tied 5 mm past the hook eye on a 1-cm finishing nail <11>
Tail: rabbit zonker strip, black
Body: dubbing, Arizona Simi-seal, colour bloody leech; comb before the wing application <37>

Wing: rabbit zonker strip black; extend even with the tail

Collar: black ostrich herl; 3–4 turns behind the bead <10>

Comment: Alternative bead, body and rabbit colours are gold/olive, copper/brown, black/black, or silver/black. Another effective balanced leech pattern is the Ruby-Eyed, a favourite of Don Freschi of Sport Fishing on the Fly (see photo). Tie it in the same manner as above using a red glass bead, claret red marabou tail, Arizona Simi-seal dubbing and a palmered black hackle.

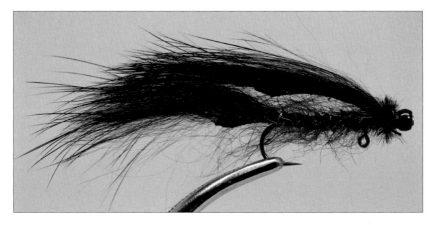

Balanced Blood Leech

Ruby-eyed Balanced Leech

Chironomids and Midges

These insects belong to the same order, Diptera, and family, Chironomidae; midges, however, are much smaller than chironomids, imitated on hook sizes #18–24. This family is the most important fish food in lakes, comprising up to 40 per cent of a trout's diet. This is the earliest major hatch to appear in spring, and the last to disappear in the autumn. If the trout are feeding on insects smaller than size #18, consider them to be midges. And those little clear, greenish-coloured worms your trout's gullet is often full of—those are midge larvae. I treat chironomid and midge tying with the same patterns, only much, much smaller for the midge. I cover this in detail in the section on creeks and rivers.

When I began to tie flies in the early 1970s under the tutelage of Jack Shaw, chironomids were my first true lessons after I learned to tie the woolly worm. Jack sent me back to the vise many times before he accepted what I had to offer. It was all about correct proportions, the key factor any good fly tyer should look to achieve with his or her dressings—*size* and *shape* again! I remember Jack's words to me as clear as day: "That will catch fish, but try it again this way...."

Chironomids display three stages of life: larva, pupa and adult. I developed the translucent bloodworm pattern in 2004, using an under-wrap of dental floss to achieve the transparent look I was after, and try as I may, I have not seen anything that improves the fly except a refined hackling method. Pupae are a different story. They are certainly the most-imitated insect stages of the past forty years, and the dressings are endless—all to achieve the four principles of size, shape, colour and movement. Many fly-tyers get everything right except movement, and though they all catch fish, I enjoy putting attitude into my pupae, hence the throat hackle, which also imitates prominent wing segments on this insect that most tyers omit.

A good emerger pattern can be very successful during a strong chironomid hatch, especially when trout are "smutting"—raising small dimples on the water as they feed on ascending pupae slightly below the water's surface or those stuck in the film. I tie emerger patterns by using the same method for chironomids, midges, mayflies and traveller sedges, varying sizes and colours to define the insect I am imitating.

Chironomid Larva (Bloodworm)

Hook: Tiemco 200R #10–18

Thread: UTC 70, black

Underbody: flat waxed dental floss; wrapped down and up the hook shank <4>

Ribs (2): single strand of red floss and fine gold wire wrapped up the shank over the underbody, followed by 1 or 2 coats of Sally Hansen's nail polish <3, 4>

Collar 1: small reddish pheasant neck feather; 4–6 strands over the body to suggest movement <8>

Collar 2: black ostrich herl; 2–3 turns <10>

Comment: Sally Hansen's takes a few minutes to set over waxed dental floss—I tie a batch and let it set for five minutes before I apply the collars.

Chironomid Larva (Bloodworm)

Chironomid Pupa, Black and Red

Hook: Tiemco 200R #12–18

Thread: UTC 70, dark grey

Bead: black 3/32 tungsten <11>

Gills: white Glo Yarn in front of the bead <34>

Ribs: X-small red wire; 8–10 counter-wraps over the abdomen <3, 4>

Abdomen: black Holographic tinsel wrapped over the underbody, followed by ribs <3, 4>

Underbody: single strand black floss; built to a cone shape <4>

Throat hackle: small red-orange cock pheasant neck feather <8>
Collar: 3–4 turns of black ostrich herl <10>

Comment: Alternative colours for abdomen, ribs and bead head are all black, black/silver/silver, black/copper/copper, brown/copper/copper, carrot orange/copper/copper, or olive/gold/gold. My "chromie" is tied with Flashabou, colour "gun metal."

After setting the bead and gills, tie in together the ribs and abdomen tinsel, take them down the shank, and then build the underbody. Bring the abdomen and ribs to the front of the hook in order. Apply 1 coat of Sally Hansen's to the abdomen and ribs, let set until dry and then finish the fly with hackle and collar.

Chironomid Pupa, Black and Red

Chironomid Emerger

Hook: Tiemco 2487 #14–18
Thread: UTC 70, dark grey
Tail (as shuck): mallard flank, colour dun, body length; tie below the hook bend with a downwards extension <9>
Ribs: fine gold wire over the abdomen <3, 4>
Abdomen: 2 natural grey goose primary barbs <45>
Wing-case: short, fine deer hairs, body length <12>
Thorax: dubbing, Stillwater Sparkle, black <37>

Comment: Alternative abdomen colours, all with gold wire, are olive, brown, or tan. After the abdomen step, tie in the deer hair at the shank mid-point; apply the thorax, pull deer hair over the thorax and finish the fly.

Chironomid Emerger

Chironomid Adult

Hook: Mustad R43 #14–16 for "bombers"; Mustad R50 #18–24 for midges

Thread: UTC 70, dark grey

Tail: fine natural deer hairs, half the body length <12>

Wing-case (as shellback): deer hairs, body length; pulled over the abdomen <41>

Abdomen: 2 goose primary barbs, natural colour <45>

Hackle: grizzly saddle; 4–5 turns <13>

Comment: Alternative colours for the abdomens are reddish brown cock pheasant sword; and tan, olive and chartreuse (midge) goose primary.

Chironomid Adult

Mayflies

Where would a fly tyer be without the mayfly, the most celebrated and mimicked insect of all time? There are over 700 species in the mayfly family; the concoctions that tyers dream up at the vise are endless. In still water lakes, however, mayflies are dominated by the insect genera Callibaetis and Caenis—these are the two classes that I imitate for my lake fishing. Caenis nymph and adult species are differentiated from Callibaetis by their sizes; use hook sizes #14–18 for Caenis, #10–14 for Callibaetis.

Mayflies have an incomplete life cycle of egg, nymph and adult, omitting the pupa stage. The adult phase, however, has two stages, dun and spinner. Duns hatch underwater or on the surface, depending on weather and wind, travel to the shoreline and within a few days trans-form into spinners, which in turn mate and fertilize females, then return to the lake to deposit their eggs. Both male and female genders die soon after the mating and egg-laying processes are completed.

My favourite nymph pattern is based on the pheasant tail version so widely imitated, but as Jack Shaw noticed during his home aquarium studies of mayfly nymphs as they prepared for mating, the colouration of their thoraxes and wing-cases darkens. These are the nymphs we wish to replicate, hence my different approach to tying the pattern using a dark wing-case and thorax. Have you also noticed that swimming nymphs travel with outstretched legs? Why then use a throat hackle to imitate legs? I prefer to "leg" my swimming/hatching nymphs with hackles that suggest this frantic action.

The mayfly emerger tie is a suggestion of an insect stuck in the surface film that is in the process of hatching—not quite complete; its nymphalid shuck and abdomen hangs underwater while the wings are drying, a perfect, easy target for cruising trout. Have you noticed that an emerging mayfly's wet wings look reddish in colour, turning grey once dried? Fish might....

Over the years I have imitated adult mayflies mostly in the tradi-tional style: hackle fibre tails, smooth bodies, upright wings and dry-style, upright hackles. In the last five years, I have dropped all that and for still waters tie an extended body mayfly that has been enormously successful for me, using only deer hair and a thorax dubbing without hackle, presenting an emerged insect which lays enticingly in the surface film.

Mayfly Callibaetis Nymph

Hook: Tiemco 100 #12–14

Thread: UTC 70, brown

Tail ball: 2–3 turns pheasant tail sword barbs at hook bend <39>

Tails: 3 cock pheasant sword barbs, body lengths <39>

Ribs: fine gold wire; 4–5 turns over the abdomen <3, 4>

Abdomen: 3–4 cock pheasant sword barbs; wrapped to the shank midpoint <45>

Wing-case: 3 peacock herls, tied at mid-point; laid over the thorax and legs to finish the fly

Legs: small brownish and speckled grouse feather; laid over the thorax <14>

Thorax: dubbing, Stillwater Sparkle, dark summer duck <37>

Comment: Alternative tail, body, leg and thorax colours for nymphs are olive, tan and grey. Caenis nymphs are common in all of these paler colours. For thoraxes, use a sparkle dubbing darker than the abdomen's colour.

Mayfly Callibaetis Nymph

Mayfly Callibaetis Emerger

Hook: Tiemco 2487 #12–14

Tail (as shuck): mallard feather, colour wood duck; body length, pointing downwards from hook bend <9>

Ribs: fine gold wire; 4–5 turns over the abdomen <3, 4>

Abdomen: 3–4 pheasant sword fibres; wrapped to the mid-point <45>

Wing-case: medium natural deer hair fibres, body length; lay over thorax, wing tips up at the head <12>

Thorax: dubbing, Stillwater Sparkle, dark summer duck <37>

Comment: Alternative colours for tail, abdomen and thorax are dun/ grey olive/ Stillwater Sparkle dub, olive. The Caenis species is imitated with size #14 hooks, and is most common in paler colours like tan and grey olive.

Mayfly Callibaetis Emerger

Mayfly Callibaetis Dun No-hackle

Hook: Mustad R43 #12–14

Thread: UTC 70, brown

Tails: 3 Mayfly Tails, colour tan, slightly longer than the full shank

Extended abdomen: 6–8 long medium deer hairs, dyed cinnamon brown <12, 16>

Wing: fine, short deer hairs; body length, dyed smoky grey <12, 15>

Thorax: dubbing, Stillwater Sparkle, dark summer duck <37>

Comment: Alternative colours for tail, abdomen and thorax are olive/grey olive/medium olive; tan/natural deer/dark summer duck.

Mayfly Callibaetis Dun No-hackle

Mayfly Callibaetis Spinner No-hackle

Hook: Mustad R43 #12–14
Thread: UTC 70, dark grey
Tails: 3 Mayfly Tails, colour light dun, slightly longer than the full shank
Extended abdomen: 6–8 long, medium deer hairs dyed black or dark grey <12, 16>
Wing: fine, short deer hairs; body length, dyed smoky grey <12, 15>
Thorax: dubbing, Stillwater Sparkle, black <37>

Comment: Alternative colours for tail, abdomen and thorax are olive/grey olive/medium olive or tan/natural deer/dark summer duck.

Mayfly Callibaetis Spinner No-hackle

Mayfly Callibaetis Spent Spinner

Hook: Mustad R43 #12–14
Thread: UTC 70, dark grey
Tails: 3 Mayfly Tails, colour light dun, slightly longer than the full shank
Extended abdomen: 6–8 deer hairs, long, dyed black or dark grey <12, 16>
Spent wing: Antron, light dun; 8–10 fibres, body length; cross-wrapped on top of the shank, splayed <33>
Thorax: dubbing, Stillwater Sparkle, black <37>

Comment: Alternative colours for tail, abdomen and thorax are olive/grey olive/medium olive or tan/natural deer/dark summer duck (Caenis).

Mayfly Callibaetis Spent Spinner

Mayfly Caenis Dun No-hackle

Hook: Mustad R43 #14–16

Thread: UTC 70, tan

Tails: 3 Mayfly Tails, colour tan, slightly longer than the full shank

Extended abdomen: 6–8 medium, natural deer hairs <12, 16>

Wing: deer hairs, fine and short, body length, natural with light tips <15>

Thorax: dubbing, Stillwater Sparkle Callibaetis, tan <37>

Comment: Alternative colours for tail and abdomen are olive and grey olive. The "spent" stage of the Caenis is tied the same as Callibaetis, using natural deer and Antron fibres.

Mayfly Caenis Dun No-hackle

Caddisflies

If there is one fly I can call my favourite for lake or stream, it's the adult caddisfly. A number of years ago, I decided to spend the rest of my fly-fishing days concentrating on fishing the surface with dry flies first, resorting to wet flies only if I had to. On numerous lakes, this meant rising at first light to catch early feeding times and being on the water for last light to capitalize on the evening's action. To my surprise, however, daylight hours between 10:00 a.m. and 3:00 p.m. were exceptional for the dry fly *if* I could locate surface activity, and pretty good otherwise for using the dry fly as a searching pattern, concentrating on shoal and drop-off areas. The adult caddisfly traveller is by far my most productive floating pattern in still water, fooling at least 80 per cent of the hundreds of trout that come to my dry flies each year. The results were no different in moving waters, but the most fruitful caddisflies were much smaller, my best days late in summer season on size #20s.

Caddisfly larvae build a home of random sticks and loose vegetation. As they grow and mature, they need to seek and rebuild new premises as their bodies grow larger. These free-swimming caddisfly larvae have long been imitated by the woolly worm pattern, a simple combination of chenille and palmered hackle, to which I add a twist of long pheasant rump to give it additional life and movement. When the larvae mature, they pupate within their cased homes, leave their encased shells and begin their journeys to the lake's surface, where they then hatch into their adult forms.

All stages of caddisfly insects are delectable trout food, but the pupa stage, though short-lived, can be hugely successful when caddisflies are hatching on the shoals. The pupae will often swim the course of the lake just under the surface, posturing for its transformation to adulthood. It's a delightful time for the fly fisher if you recognize this stage, as floating or intermediate lines are ideal for this pre-hatch activity, trout slamming the ascending pupa with great vigour and glee.

The caddisfly adult traveller that I tie is an off-shoot of the venerable Mikulak Sedge that fly-fishing pioneer Art Mikulak developed and popularized in the 1980s. I've added my own twists to the pattern: using deer hair instead of elk, longer wing extensions, front hackles mixed grizzly and brown; however, it is the Mikulak style that I've captured, and for me this is the most successful dry fly in my box because I can use it any time as my prime searching pattern, hatch or no hatch in progress. As an alternative, my down-wing caddisfly style is very effective for imitating small caddisflies sizes #14–16 that hatch from still water.

Caddisfly Larva Traveller

Hook: Mustad R75 #6–12
Thread: UTC 70, olive
Underbody: .020 mm lead wire; 10–12 wraps at mid-shank <5>
Ribs: grizzly olive hackle; palmered over the body and trimmed to the hook gape <17>
Body: Krystal chenille, olive <3, 10>
Collar: pheasant rump, bluish-green, 1.5X body length <8>
Head: 2–3 peacock herls; twisted and wrapped in front of the collar <22>

Comment: Alternative body and hackle colours are tan/brown, black/grizzly, dark olive/olive, or Naples yellow/ginger.

Caddisfly Larva Traveller

Caddisfly Pupa Traveller

Hook: Tiemco 200R #6–14

Thread: UTC 70, olive

Underbody: .020 mm lead wire; 10–12 wraps at the rear of the shank <5>

Ribs: rod building thread, yellow <3, 4>

Abdomen: dubbing, Stillwater Sparkle, olive <37>

Thorax: dubbing, Stillwater Sparkle Callibaetis tan <37>

Swimmerets (as legs): golden pheasant tippet feather applied as throat hackle; spread them <8>

Collar: pheasant rump feather, bluish-green, 1.5X body length <8>

Head: 3 peacock herls twisted and wrapped 3 times at the head <22>

Comment: Alternative body, ribs and thorax colours are tan/bright green/olive, grey/bright green/olive, or Naples yellow/bright green/olive.

Caddisfly Pupa Traveller

Caddisfly Emerger Traveller

Hook: Tiemco 2487 #8–12

Thread: UTC 70, olive

Tail 1(as swimmerets): golden pheasant tippet feather; body length, swept downward <9>

Tail 2 (as shuck): mallard flank feather dyed olive; swept past the swimmerets <9>

Ribs: rod building thread, yellow <3, 4>

Wing-case: medium natural deer hair fibres, body length; after the thorax application, lay them over the thorax, wing tips upright at the head <12>

Thorax: dubbing, Stillwater Sparkle Callibaetis tan <37>

Comment: Alternative body, ribs and thorax colours are tan/bright green/olive, grey/bright green/olive, or Naples yellow/bright green/olive.

Caddisfly Emerger Traveller

Caddisfly Adult Traveller

Hook: Mustad R43 #6–12
Thread: UTC 140, tan
Tail: deer or elk hairs, natural long and coarse, half body length <12>
Body: dubbing, Haretron Plus HT2 dark hare's ear <37>
Wings: deer or elk hairs, natural long and coarse; 4 stacks between 2–3 turns of body dubbing <12, 18>
Antennae (2) (optional): black boar bristles, curled <20>
Hackles: grizzly and brown or dun; 3–4 turns of each <13>

Comment: Alternative body colours are caddisfly green, olive dun, tan, or cinnamon; a lime green dubbing egg sack under the tail at the butt for egg-laying imitations. This is my improvised version of the Mikulak Sedge, designed by the late Art Mikulak in the 1980s. For over twenty years, it has worked on every lake and stream I've tried it. An amazing caddisfly pattern! Sometimes you have to *create* a hatch on lakes and streams—flog the water with multiple casts until fish *think* something is going on—this is the pattern to do it with in still water.

Caddisfly Adult Traveller

Caddisfly Adult Small Down-wing

Hook: Mustad R43 #14–18
Thread: UTC 70, tan
Hackle 1: saddle hackle, dun; palmer over the body; trim flat on top of the body <17>
Body: dubbing, Stillwater Sparkle Callibaetis tan <37>
Underwing: CDC feather, dyed tan <40>
Overwing: pheasant wing primary feather slip; folded in half over the body and underwing <19>
Antennae (2): tan marabou stems <20>
Hackle 2: saddle hackle, dun; 4–5 turns <13>

Comment: This is my pattern for all of the *small* caddisflies (hook sizes #14–18) that hatch from still water. Alternative body and saddle hackle colours are olive/dun, cinnamon/brown, or pale yellow/ginger.

Caddisfly Adult Small Down-wing

Damselfly Nymph

Oh my, the damselfly! During annual late spring and autumn migrations of nymphs to and from deeper water and shallow shoals, usually a two-week period at both ends, this nymph is noticed and consumed greedily by foraging trout. Normally shy insects that hide from their predators in weedy vegetation, damselfly larvae travel to the shoals in mass numbers to mate some time between mid-May and mid-June, depending upon the elevation of the lake. They climb and attach themselves to bulrushes, reeds and boat docks to emerge and then seek to propagate. The reverse migration occurs during late autumn, when the young of the year return to deep, warmer water to overwinter.

Jack Shaw's damselfly nymph tie of the 1970s inspired my model. I've tinkered with the pattern for years: added bead heads, used marabou for swimming action, and played with colours, but in the final summation, it's hard to beat Jack's original for appearance and movement, although I have altered his materials to suit my own tying style. I've added tail appendages, using hackle tips to suggest the impression of the rudders that damselflies use for propulsion and steering, leg hackles that suggest outstretched movement and more definitive eyeballs, which are a key characteristic of damselfly nymphs.

Adult damselflies, characterized by their bright blue (male) or olive green (female) bodies banded with black, live for several months, until

Damselfly Nymph—Jack Shaw original

the first heavy frosts of autumn, and they can mate several times during their short life, but are not often caught and consumed by fish.

Damselfly Nymph

Hook: Tiemco 200R #8–12
Thread: UTC 70, grey brown
Dubbing ball: pale olive ostrich herls <39>
Tails: 2 badger hackle tips, half the abdomen lengths; each side of the dubbing ball <21>
Ribs: fine gold wire; 5–6 turns counter-wrapped for strength <3, 4>
Abdomen: 2–3 pale olive ostrich herls, applied in dubbing hook <22>
Wing-case: olive primary feather fibres; laid over the thorax, legs and head
Legs: small grouse feather, olive; lay it over the thorax <14>
Head: Larva Lace, olive; cross-wrapped behind the hook eye; burned to length, over-wrapped with 2–3 ostrich herls, pale olive <23>
Thorax: 2–3 ostrich herls, pale olive; continued from the head wrapping <22>

Comment: Alternative colours for the abdomen, thorax and legs are dark olive/ olive; tan/ brown; Naples yellow/ brown.

Damselfly Nymph

Dragonfly Nymph

Dragonfly nymphs are predators of the still water ponds and lakes, hunting and consuming every order of insect in their paths. Other than mature leeches, which are primarily vegetarians, and the giant water beetle, dragons are the largest insect that swims in lakes. There are two species that are important to imitate when tying flies: darners, the largest, which are longer and more slender than their cousins; and the red-shouldered nymphs, which are short, paler in colour than darners, and are very squat and robust looking. As adults, darners are the big boys, reaching up to 80 mm in length. As flying adults, they appear long and trim in radiant colours of blue, green and mixed brown. The red-shouldered adult, often mistaken for and called the Gomphus, matures at 50 mm in length, and does have red shoulder bands, displaying abdomen colours of brown and olive green. Both nymphs' young-of-the-year is a necessary insect for autumn fishing, so you need to tie dragonfly nymphs as small as size #14.

The most difficult feature to imitate with both insects is their shape, and you really need to work at it to get the proportions correct. For the darner, I use a 5X-long hook, and build the back end of the nymph first with an underbody of lead wire, followed by at least 3 wraps of embroidery thread over the lead wire; I'll then crush the body flat with non-serrated pliers, constructing an underbody that is a teardrop in appearance. I repeat this procedure for the red-shouldered nymph, but tie the pattern on a 2X-long hook. Both insects have dominant eyes; it's very important to include these in your recipe.

Darner Dragonfly Nymph

Hook: Mustad R75 #6–14
Thread: UTC 70, olive
Tail: moose hairs; short, to imitate an appendage
Ribs: medium copper wire; 6–8 turns over the abdomen <3, 4>
Underbody 1: .025 mm lead wire; apply to the rear half of the shank, flattened after underbody 2 is applied <5>
Underbody 2: olive embroidery thread; 3 wraps back and forth over underbody 1; crush <27>

Abdomen: dubbing, Stillwater Sparkle, dark olive green <37>
Wing-case: dark turkey primary fibres, folded
Legs: grouse wing feather, brown phase; lay over the thorax <14>
Eyes: black dumbbells, or glass beads on 20 lb. test mono; wrap with peacock herls <26>
Thorax: 3–4 peacock herls in dubbing loop <22>
Collar: 2–3 turns of ostrich herls, grey <10>

Comment: Alternative abdomen and legs colours are medium olive/olive or olive grey/pale olive (sizes #12–14).

Darner Dragonfly Nymph

Red-shouldered Dragonfly Nymph

Hook: Mustad R73 #8–14
Thread: UTC 70, grey brown
Tail: short moose hairs, as an appendage
Ribs: medium gold wire; 5–6 turns over the abdomen <3, 4>
Underbody 1: .020 mm lead wire; 8–10 wraps at the rear half of the shank; flatten after underbody 2 is applied <5>
Underbody 2: embroidery thread, olive; 3 wraps back and forth over underbody 1; crush <27>
Abdomen: dubbing, SCD 259 olive scud <37>
Wing-case: olive primary fibres, folded

Legs: grouse wing feather, dyed olive; lay over the thorax <14>

Eyes: black dumbbells, or glass beads on 20 lb. test mono; wrap with peacock herls <26>

Thorax: 3–4 peacock herls in dubbing loop <22>

Collar: 2–3 turns of ostrich herls, grey <10>

Comment: Alternative abdomen/legs colours are tan/brown, pale olive/olive (sizes #12–14) or Naples yellow/brown.

Red-shouldered Dragonfly Nymph

Dragonfly Nymph—Jack Shaw original

Water Boatman and Backswimmer

During my fifty years of fly fishing, I can count on two hands the number of days that I have caught the boatman "hatch," or what I refer to as their mating flights; however, the good days have been memorable to the point that I look for it every autumn. Weather conditions need to be perfect: late August-September, clear mid-afternoon, first frosts and no wind—a hint of autumn stillness in the air. More often than not, the conditions can be ideal, just as described, but the flight doesn't come....

I have tinkered with this fly pattern for fifty years, but have now succumbed to a simple tie of chenille, legs and dominant eyes. Krystal chenille over-wrapped with plastic simulates the insect body, the flashiness of the material faking the bubble of air the insect carries for breathing purposes; peacock herl represents the hairy-looking propulsion oars the beetles use to swim. It doesn't seem to matter if you tie the backswimmer to swim upside down. Both insects move quickly through the water column, a plop on the surface and flash of silver—trout attack them with reckless abandon on random days for a few weeks every year.

Water Boatman

Hook: Tiemco 100 #12–14
Thread: UTC 70, tan
Wing-case: barred pheasant sword fibres; pulled over the body and eyes
Over-wrap: 3 mm Midge Flex; apply over the body as a rib
Underbody: at mid-shank, build with tan embroidery thread <27>
Eyes: brown V-rib; body width, burned <23>
Body: small gold Krystal chenille; over-wrap with clear Midge Flex <3>
Oars: peacock sword, more than full body lengths; insert at the midpoint of the body with a darning needle; Super Glue where it enters the body; trim longer than the body length

Comment: Apply in the order listed; after finishing, apply two coats of flexible cement or one coat of 5-minute epoxy to the wing-cases. If needed, apply bars on the wing-cases with a black Sharpie marker when they are dry.

Alternative body colours: dark green peacock herls, pearl Krystal chenille.

Water Boatman

Backswimmer

Hook: Tiemco 100 #8–10

Thread: UTC 70, dark grey

Wing-case: barred pheasant sword fibres, pulled over the body and eyes

Over-wrap: 3 mm Midge Flex; apply over the body as a rib

Underbody: at the mid-shank, build with grey embroidery thread <27>

Eyes: brown V-rib; body width, burned <23>

Body: small pearl Krystal chenille; over-wrap with clear Midge Flex <3>

Oars: peacock sword, more than the full body length; insert at the mid-point with a darning needle; Super Glue where it enters the body, and trim longer than the body length

Comment: Apply in the order listed. After finishing, apply two coats of flexible cement or one coat of 5-minute epoxy to the wing-cases. If needed, apply bars on the wing-cases with a Sharpie marker when they are dry.

Backswimmer

Terrestrials

Insects that hatch or travel from land to lake can be important match-the-hatch bugs for still water fishing because they are available for short periods of time and are considered a dessert item for trout: they don't come often, awaken the taste buds differently than their ordinary table fare does, and spur aggressive feeding behaviour. For the fly fisher, being in the right place at the right time is everything, since this only happens once or twice a season. The fisher person's bragging axiom "You should have been here yesterday" applies often with terrestrial movements of still water fishing.

If you fish lakes surrounded with an abundance of cottonwood and aspen trees, the annual colonizing flights of red, black and huge carpenter ants will be a key target to watch for during your summer fishing ventures. Conditions need to be right, with a nice warm day and a bit of breezy weather, but if you hit the "hatch" as bugs are blown onto the lake, you are a blessed person.

Hoppers fall into the same random opportunities as ants; if your lake has grassy meadows lining the banks, you are in hopper country, and can often take your largest trout of the day by hunting the shoreline with a hopper pattern on a warm, blustery afternoon.

A mouse pattern is essential for a complete terrestrial offering. The little creatures roam the banks of all lakes and streams, sometimes slipping off the bank while nosing around for their meals. In their panicked haste to get back to shore, they will often swim in the wrong direction to the middle of the lake—tough luck!

Black Flying Ant

Hook: Tiemco 100 #12–18
Thread: UTC 70, black
Wing-case: strip of black foam, 2 mm in width <28>
Abdomen: dubbing, Haretron Plus HT-7, black <37>
Wing: CDC feather natural; lay it over the abdomen <40>
Hackle: saddle, black; 3–4 turns <13>
Thorax: black foam; smaller than the wing-case

Comment: Alternative colours for the wing-case, abdomen, hackle and thorax: are black/black/black/orange and orange/burnt orange/brown/orange. The carpenter ant is tied all-black/natural wing on size #8–10 hooks.

Black Flying Ant

Hopper

Hook: Mustad R43 #6–12
Thread: UTC 140, hopper yellow
Tail: red calf tail hairs; half the body length
Abdomen 1: foam strips, 3 mm, brown over yellow; extend to the tail length <28>
Hackle: brown; palmered over abdomen 2; top hackle fibres are trimmed flat <17>
Abdomen 2: dubbing, Haretron 15, pale olive <37>
Legs: Legs-on-a-Stick (2); length of abdomen 2 <29>
Overwing: mottled turkey; lay flat over abdomens 1 and 2; fold and trim <19>
Head: spun deer hairs dyed light olive, trimmed square <30>

Comment: Alternative abdomen foam colours: brown over tan, green over yellow.

Hopper

Mouse

Hook: Mustad R43 #4–6

Thread: UTC 140, tan

Tail: marabou plume, body length <9>

Body: spun and stacked deer hair; trimmed flat on bottom, oval on top and sides, smaller at the head; clip flat spots on the sides of the head for eyes <12, 18, 30>

Legs: brown Sili legs, tied at the two-thirds point of the shank; extend to the rear of the tail

Eyes: tape-on eyes, black on silver; cement to the head's flat spots with Super Glue

Mouse

Minnow Imitations

In many still waters, especially those in the northern half of our province where natural orders of fish propagation occur and there is no need for fisheries stocking programs, minnows and smolts form a significant percentage of a fish's diet, especially for trout of the Blackwater strain. These indigenous minnow species include northern pike minnows, migrating sockeye smolts and yearling fry, when a lake supports a summer sockeye run, whitefish fry, rainbow trout fry, shiners, and in the case of Quesnel's Dragon Lake, illegally introduced goldfish, which are prospering in the lake's rich aquatic environment. Trout prey on 2–4-cm minnows most of the time, newly hatched fry that are easy to catch because they swim poorly and are naïve, having not yet learned avoidance tactics like where to hide.

Minnow fry imitations representing the young-of-the-year of different species have common characteristics that need to be reproduced in your patterns. Smolt patterns, year-old migrating minnows, are tied the same as minnows except they are much larger, up to 8 cm, and can be tied on a shank with a trailing hook to increase length. Common features of minnow fry and smolts are: 4-X streamer hooks; pearl, silver or gold bodies; flash to complement the body; white polar bear, calf or bucktail hairs to simulate flanks; olive, grey, or bright green hairs or marabou feather topping to simulate their back colours; and dominant eyes.

The secret to tying good-looking minnow imitations is to keep materials sparse and streamlined on the shank—the streamer needs to flow, dart and undulate in the water with every movement you impart: short strips, long pulls, and pauses.

Marabou Goldfish Minnow

Hook: Mustad R75 #4–12
Thread: UTC 140, white
Rib: silver wire; 5–6 counter-wraps over the body <3, 4>
Body: pearl Mylar wrapped down and back; coat the ribs and body with flexible cement for strength <3>
Belly: polar bear hairs, white; sparse <46>
Flash: pearl Flashabou; 3 strands doubled, belly length <33>

Overwing 1: polar bear hairs, white; sparse <46>
Overwing 2: marabou fibres, fluorescent yellow; sparse <8>
Overwing 3: marabou feather, hot orange; 2:1 ratio to overwings 1 and
2 <8>
Eyes: painted, black on yellow <31>

Comment: Alternative colours for bodies and overwing 3 are silver/
black, gold/olive and gold/brown, silver/grey. This orange tie is what I
use at Dragon Lake to imitate goldfish, presented in size #10.

Marabou Goldfish Minnow

Marabou Pike Minnow

Hook: Mustad R75 #4–12
Thread: UTC 140, white
Rib: silver wire; 5–6 counter-wraps over the body <3, 4>
Body: pearl Mylar wrapped down and back; coat the ribs and body with flexible cement for strength <3>
Belly: polar bear hairs, white; sparse <46>
Flash: pearl Flashabou; 3 strands doubled, belly length <33>
Overwing 1: polar bear hairs, white; sparse <46>
Overwing 2: marabou fibres, chartreuse; sparse <8>
Overwing 3: marabou feather, olive; 2:1 ratio to overwings 1 and 2 <8>
Eyes: painted, black on yellow <31>

Marabou Pike Minnow

General Imitations

Where would a fishing life be without a few of those patterns that either imitate everything edible, like the Bulldog, or a fly that evokes aggression, like the Booby? The Bulldog was originated and named by my friend Brent Schlenker of Medicine Hat, Alberta, for our mutual friend Dale Freschi (the Bulldog) of *Sport Fishing on the Fly* fame, whereas the Booby was imported from England. Dale and his brother Don, however, made both of these flies famous and popular in North America through their WFN show, *Sport Fishing on the Fly*. Both patterns are now considered staples in a fly fisher's arsenal, and are especially effective for enticing moody trout during periods of non-hatch activity on lakes and rivers.

Bulldog

Hook: Mustad R75 #4–10
Thread: UTC 70, black
Tail: marabou feather, burnt orange; body length <9>
Hackles (2): grizzly olive and grizzly burnt orange (olive is shorter); palmer both over the body <17>
Body: gold Krystal chenille, medium <3, 10>

Bulldog

Tequila Booby

Hook: Tiemco 2457 #8–10
Thread: UTC 140, burnt orange
Tail: marabou feather, fluorescent yellow, trimmed short <9>
Body 1: Fritz chenille, fluorescent yellow; 2 turns <10>
Eyes: booby eyes, white, at the hook eye <32>
Body 2: Fritz chenille, fluorescent orange; 4–5 turns <10>

Comment: These "boobies" can be tied in a number of colours: black, purple, red and claret.

Tequila Booby

ESSENTIAL TROUT FLIES FOR CREEKS AND RIVERS

Midges

Midges comprise up to 50 per cent of a fish's diet in streams. For a fly tyer who fishes lakes more often than rivers and creeks, he/she has a head start on tying this pattern, because the four life stages of a midge for stream fishing can be duplicated by tying still water chironomids several sizes smaller. One pattern I treat a bit differently is the midge larva stage, which is a simple tie of Larva Lace ribbed with red wire on a small hook, because the fly needs to sink rapidly and bounce along the streambed to be effective.

The pupa, emerger and adult stages of midges are well represented on sizes #18–24 hooks. When tying them, I cut my materials amounts drastically compared to still water chironomids, but continue to focus on size and some form of motion. The midge adult phase is where one of the most popular dry flies of all time is presented—the Adams, a general pattern revered by many fly fishers as the ultimate emerging midge/mayfly imitation.

Midge Larva

Hook: Tiemco 200 #16–20
Thread: UTC 70, dark grey
Ribs: X-small red wire <3, 4>
Body: Larva Lace, red, smallest; coat with flexible cement after the ribs are applied <3, 4>
Collar 1: small reddish pheasant neck feather <8>
Collar 2: 2–3 turns of black ostrich herl <10>

Comment: Alternative body colours are olive, tan, cream and black.

Midge Larva

Midge Pupa

Hook: Tiemco 2457 #18–20
Thread: UTC 70, dark grey
Gills: white Glo Yarn <34>
Ribs: fine silver wire; 4–5 turns over the abdomen <3, 4>
Abdomen: tying threads; build to a cone shape, then coat with flexible cement after the ribs are applied
Throat: small reddish-orange pheasant neck feather <8>
Collar: 2–3 turns of black ostrich herl <10>

Comment: Alternative abdomen/collar colours are olive/olive; brown/ brown; or lime green/olive.

Midge Pupa

Midge Emerger

Hook: Tiemco 2487 #18–20
Thread: UTC 70, dark grey
Tail (as shuck): mallard feather, dun colour <9>
Ribs: fine gold wire; 4–5 turns over the abdomen <3, 4>
Abdomen: single grey goose primary barb <45>
Wing-case: fine deer hairs with light tips; lay these over the thorax <12>
Thorax: dubbing, Stillwater Sparkle, black <37>

Comment: Alternative abdomen/thorax colours are olive/dark olive; brown/dark brown; or lime green/olive.

Midge Emerger

Midge Adult

Hook: Tiemco 101 #18–24
Thread: UTC 70, dark grey
Tail (as shuck): fine deer hairs <41>
Wing-case: fine deer hairs; lay these over the body <41>
Body: 2 goose primary barbs, natural grey <45>
Hackle: grizzly; 3–4 turns <13>

Comment: Alternative body colours are olive, brown, tan, black and lime green.

Midge Adult

Traditional Adams

Hook: Tiemco 101 #14–22
Thread: UTC 70, dark grey
Tail: grizzly and brown mixed, shank length <9>
Wings: 2 grizzly hackle tips body length, upright and divided <35>
Body: dubbing, natural rabbit <37>
Hackles: grizzly and brown mixed <13>

Traditional Adams

Mayflies

Unlike lakes, where only a few species of mayflies exist, creeks, rivers and streams will support a host of families that hatch at different times of the year or, in most cases, overlap with each other, creating a confusing myriad of choices for the fly fisher. The best way to approach match-the-hatch selections for insects in moving water is by observing their sizes and colours, and having an assortment to offer the fish. Turning over some rocks will expose the fish's underwater menu, lending clues to what is hatching on the surface.

Mayfly nymphs are basic table fare for fish, available year-round, and are good examples of this *match the size* theory: use a bead head pheasant tail nymph in sizes #10–16 for large drakes and smaller mayflies, and a bead head little grey nymph in sizes #14–18 for everything else, including small stoneflies. The key ingredient for nymph design is to enhance it with weight so it tumbles along the bottom of the stream; tying your flies with 2X strong hooks and adding tungsten beads to the heads solves this problem.

Mayfly emerger patterns are very good imitations of the stuck-in-the-shuck, helpless attitude of mayflies evolving in fast water, because the river's current inhibits their quick getaway to safe environs. I developed my emerger design around 2005 while on a cutthroat fishing expedition with my sons in southern Alberta—it has been wildly successful for me and led me to repeat the model for all of the emerging insects that hatch in the water: chironomid, midge, caddisfly and mayfly.

Next to caddisflies, the short-lived mayfly adults are my second favourite dry fly choice. I tie variations of the adult stage in four colours and several different sizes of each colour to match the hatches I see. For streams, you can match all of the hatches with four abdomen deer hair colours in hook sizes #12–24: cinnamon brown 10–14 for brown drakes; olive grey 12–18 for green drakes, flavs and blue-winged olives; natural tan in sizes #14–18 for pale morning and evening duns; charcoal grey or black sizes #22–24 for tricos. For the thorax portion, choose a sparkle dubbing of the same tone but darker than the abdomen. Duns and spinners have grey-toned deer hair wings, spent spinners clear outstretched Antron fibres.

Mayfly Nymph, Pheasant Tail

Hook: Tiemco 2457 #10–16

Thread: UTC 70, brown

Bead head: gold tungsten 1/8 to 5/64 <11>

Tail ball: 2–3 cock pheasant sword tail barbs; 2–3 wraps below the hook bend to separate the tails <39>

Tails: 3 pheasant sword barb tips; abdomen length, on top of the tail ball <39>

Ribs: medium gold wire; 4–5 turns counter-wrapped over the abdomen for strength <3, 4>

Abdomen: 3–4 pheasant sword barbs wrapped to the mid-point of the shank <45>

Wing-case: 3–4 peacock herls; lay them over the thorax and legs

Legs: small reddish cock pheasant neck feather; lay it over the thorax <14>

Thorax: dubbing, Stillwater Sparkle, dark brown <37>

Collar: 2–3 turns of brown ostrich herl <10>

Comment: This fly is presented in size #12. For sizes #14–16, reduce your dressing materials.

Mayfly Nymph, Pheasant Tail

Mayfly Nymph, Little Grey

Hook: Tiemco 2457 #14–18
Thread: UTC 70, dark grey
Bead head: black tungsten 3/32 <11>
Tail ball: goose primary barb; 2 turns below the hook bend <39>
Tails: small goose primary biots; each side of the tail ball <39>
Ribs: fine gold wire; 3–4 turns over the abdomen <3, 4>
Abdomen: 2 grey goose primary barbs wrapped to the mid-point of the shank <45>
Wing-case: 2 peacock herls; lay them over the thorax and legs
Legs: small grey pigeon wing feather; lay it over the thorax <14>
Thorax: dubbing, Stillwater Sparkle, black <37>
Collar: grey ostrich herl; 2–3 turns behind the bead <10>

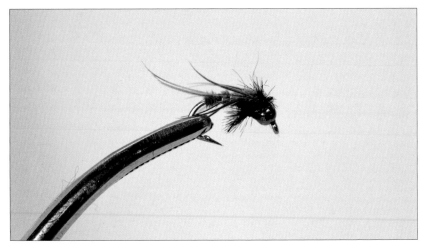

Mayfly Nymph, Little Grey

Mayfly, Green Drake Emerger

Hook: Tiemco 2487 #12–14
Thread: UTC 70, grey brown
Tail (as shuck): mallard flank feather, dark dun <9>
Ribs: fine gold wire; 4–5 turns over the abdomen <3, 4>
Abdomen: 2–3 goose primary barbs, grey olive <45>

Wing-case: medium deer hairs dyed grey olive; body length over the thorax with tips upright <12, 41>
Thorax: dubbing, Stillwater Sparkle, dark olive <37>

Comment: Alternative tail, abdomen and thorax colours to match the hatch are dun/grey/black; summer duck/brown (pheasant sword)/sparkle brown; and tan/tan/summer duck sparkle. The Blue-winged Olive Emerger is tied in the same fashion, except hook size is #16–18.

Mayfly, Green Drake Emerger

Blue-winged Olive Emerger

Mayfly, Green Drake Dun

Hook: Tiemco 101 #12–14
Thread: UTC 70, grey brown
Tail: 6–8 moose hairs slightly longer than the hook shank <36>
Abdomen: medium deer hairs dyed olive grey <16>
Wing: fine deer hairs dyed smoky grey <15>
Hackles: mixed grizzly and dun; 4–5 turns of each <13>

Comment: I tie traditional hackle-style flies for streams and rivers because I like them to float high and dry. I also carry my no-hackle and parachute versions of mayflies to the stream because you never know...

Mayfly, Green Drake Dun

Mayfly, Green Drake Parachute

Hook: Tiemco 101 #12–14
Thread: UTC 70, grey brown
Tail: 6–8 moose hairs, slightly longer than the hook shank <36>
Abdomen: medium deer hairs dyed olive grey <16>
Wing: fine deer hairs dyed smoky grey; posted <15>
Thorax: dubbing, Stillwater Sparkle, dark olive <37>
Hackle: dun saddle; 4–5 turns around the post <38>

Mayfly, Green Drake Parachute

Mayfly, Tan No-hackle

Hook: Tiemco 101 #14–18
Thread: UTC 70, tan
Tails: 3 moose hairs slightly longer than the hook shank <36>
Abdomen: medium deer hairs, natural <16>
Wing: fine deer hairs, natural (I like light brown tips), body length only <15>
Thorax: dubbing, Stillwater Sparkle Callibaetis tan; 3 wraps behind and 2 wraps in front of the wing <37>

Comment: This is a fabulous fly that I designed over the winter of 2017–18 and tested on the Crooked River in the spring of '18 with awesome results. It sits down beautifully in soft water. Tie them in all the mayfly colours and in sizes #14–20 depending on the hatches—they should replace parachute flies in your box and are much easier to tie.

Mayfly, Tan No-hackle

Mayfly, Blue-winged Olive No-hackle

Hook: Tiemco 101 #18–20
Thread: UTC 70, tan
Tails: 3–4 moose hairs slightly longer than the hook shank <36>
Abdomen: medium deer hairs, olive <16>
Wing: fine deer hairs dyed blue-grey, body length only <15>
Thorax: dubbing, Hareline Sparkle, dark olive; 2–3 wraps behind and 2 wraps in front of the wing <37>

Comment: This is another version of my no-hackle series of mayfly patterns that has proven indispensable in soft-flowing water.

Mayfly, Blue-winged Olive No-hackle

Western Tan Adams

Hook: Tiemco 101 #14–22
Thread: UTC 70, tan
Tail: moose hairs; shank length <36>
Wing: fine deer hairs <12, 15>
Body: dubbing, natural rabbit <37>
Hackle: dun saddle; 6 turns <6, 13>

Comment: I designed this version of the Adams as a mayfly for our tumbling western waters; it has become a favourite of mine.

Western Tan Adams

Mayfly, Trico Spinner

Hook: Tiemco 101 #22–26 (presented in #22)
Thread: UTC 70, dark grey
Tails: 3 light dun Mayfly Tails, 2X body length <9>
Abdomen: tying thread coated with flex cement
Wings: Antron fibres; 1.5X body length, splayed <33>
Thorax: dubbing, Stillwater Sparkle, black <37>

Mayfly, Trico Spinner

Stoneflies

The big stoneflies hatch early in the season during spring runoff in May and June; the smaller ones, little olives and sallies, begin in June, peak a month or so later during July and are often still around in mid-August. Their hatches often overlap with midges, caddisflies and mayflies; it's quite disconcerting when you arrive at your favourite stream to see all four species flitting over the water and then trying to figure which one the fish want to choose.

The major emergences of the big guys—skwalas first and earliest in the year, Salmonflies next and then goldens—occurs during the low light conditions of twilight and early dawn, the nymphs migrating to shoreline and climbing onto logs and dry rocks to split their cases and morph into adults. The much smaller olives and sallies will hatch in the river and are well represented by the little grey nymph mayfly pattern.

Stonefly adults are huge insects, up to 5 cm long, and "stimulator" fly patterns are probably for most fly-fishers the number one searching pattern for any river system during periods of non-hatch activity—trout can't resist them, and will clobber them year-round. River trout are opportunists and this is one meal they cannot pass on. I tie two versions of skwalas, Salmonflies and golden stones adults: the down-wing, which is newly hatched and often wind-blown and lying on the surface; and the fluttering female, which has mated and returned to the river to lay her eggs. Salmonflies are the largest species; sizes #4–6 3X hooks are about right, whereas for goldens and skwalas, average hooks are sizes #8–10 3X. For the little guys—olives, sallies and the little black winter stoneflies—I prefer down-wing style patterns in sizes #14–18 3X.

Stonefly Nymph, Salmonfly

Hook: Mustad SL73 #4–8
Thread: UTC 70, black
Dubbing ball: dubbing, Haretron plus HT 7, black <39>
Tails: 2 black goose biots; applied to each side of the dubbing ball <39>
Underbody: .025 mm lead wire; 10–12 wraps at the rear of the hook, squashed to a flat, oval shape <5>
Ribs: medium copper wire; 5–6 turns over the abdomen <3, 4>

Abdomen: dubbing, Haretron plus HT 7, black <37>

Wing-case: dark turkey primary folded; at completion of the fly, lay it over the eyes and thorax <19>

Legs: pheasant neck feather dyed black; lay it over the thorax <14>

Eyes: 25 lb mono; burnt, wrapped with peacock herls after the antennae are applied <26, 22>

Antennae: 2 goose biots, black; pointed forward

Thorax: 4–5 peacock herls <22>

Collar: ostrich herls, black; 2–3 turns behind the eyes <10>

Comment: For the skwala nymph, I use a size #8 hook. I like heavy up-eye steelhead hooks for stonefly nymphs; they sink and drift well in rivers.

Stonefly Nymph, Salmonfly

Stonefly Nymph, Golden

Hook: Mustad SL73 #8–10

Thread: UTC 70, brown

Dubbing ball: dubbing, Kaufmann's KB 120, golden stone <39>

Tails: 2 brown goose biots; apply to each side of the dubbing ball <39>

Underbody: .025 mm lead wire; 10–12 wraps at the rear of the hook squashed to a flat, oval shape <5>

Ribs: medium copper wire; 5–6 turns over the abdomen <3, 4>

Abdomen: dubbing, KB 120 Kaufmann's, golden stone <37>

Wing-case: dark turkey primary folded; at the completion of the fly, lay it over the eyes and thorax <19>

Legs: pheasant neck feather, natural brown; lay it over the thorax <14>

Eyes: 25 lb mono; burnt, wrapped with peacock herls after the antennae are applied <26, 22>

Antennae: 2 brown goose biots; pointed forward

Thorax: 4–5 peacock herls <22>

Collar: brown ostrich herls; 2–3 turns behind eyes <10>

Stonefly Nymph, Golden

Stonefly Adult, Salmonfly Down-wing

Hook: Mustad R43 #4–8

Thread: UTC 70, burnt orange

Dubbing ball: dubbing, Haretron HE 17, rusty orange <39>

Tails: 2 brown goose biots <39>

Hackle 1: brown; palmered through the abdomen and trimmed flat on top <17>

Abdomen: dubbing, Haretron HE 17, rusty orange <37>

Underwing: CDC feather, rusty spinner; extend to the end of the tail biots <40>

Overwing: dark grey turkey primary folded and trimmed; extend to the end of the tails <19>

Antennae: 2 dark hackle stems; plucked <20>

Hackle 2: brown; 6–8 turns <13>

Comment: I tie the "fluttering" Salmonfly exactly the same way, except I substitute dark cow elk hairs as the overwing.

Above: Stonefly Adult, Salmonfly Down-wing

Left: Stonefly Adult, Salmonfly Fluttering

Stonefly Adult, Golden Down-wing

Hook: Mustad R43 #6–10
Thread: UTC 70, hopper yellow
Dubbing ball: dubbing, Haretron HT 10 golden stone <39>
Tails: 2 brown goose biots <39>
Hackle 1: brown; palmered through the abdomen and trimmed flat on top <17>
Abdomen: dubbing, Haretron HT 10 golden stone <37>
Underwing: CDC feather, medium grey dun; extend to the end of the tails <40>
Overwing: dark grey turkey primary folded and trimmed; extend to the end of the tails <19>
Antennae: 2 dark hackle stems; plucked <20>
Hackle 2: brown; 6–8 turns <13>

Comment: I tie my "fluttering" golden stone exactly the same, except I substitute dark cow elk hairs as the overwing. For a skwala pattern, use these same size hooks and recipes; however, substitute an abdomen of wrapped peacock herls, using tip 22.

Above: Stonefly Adult, Golden Down-wing

Left: Stonefly Adult, Golden Fluttering

Stonefly Adult, Skwala Down-wing

Stonefly Adult, Little Olive

Hook: Mustad R43 #14–16
Thread: UTC 70, olive
Hackle 1: olive; palmered through the body <17>
Body: dubbing, Stillwater Sparkle olive <37>
Underwing: CDC feather, medium dun <40>
Overwing: cock pheasant wing primary strip, olive grey; folded and tied
flat over the underwing, 1.5X body length <19>
Antennae (2): stripped black marabou plume stems <20>
Hackle 2: olive; 4–5 turns <13>

Stonefly Adult, Little Olive

Comment: This is one of my very favourite stonefly patterns—in our northern half of BC, the "little olive" hatch comes off our rivers periodically all spring and summer long, and fish will often feed on them exclusively when it happens.

Stonefly Adult, Lime Sally

Hook: Mustad R43 #16–18
Thread: Danville lime, 70 denier
Egg sack: 3 turns at the hook bend of egg-orange floss
Hackle 1: grizzly; palmered over the body; trimmed flat on top of the body <17>
Body: single strand, lime green wool or thread
Underwing: CDC feather, medium dun <40>
Overwing: cock pheasant wing primary strip, olive grey; folded over the underwing, 1.5X body length <19>
Hackle 2: grizzly; 4–5 turns <13>

Stonefly Adult, Lime Sally

Stonefly Adult, Little Winter Black

Hook: Mustad R43 #16–18
Thread: UTC 70, black
Hackle 1: black; palmered over the body and trimmed flat on top of the body <17>
Body: dubbing, Haretron HT7, black <37>
Underwing: CDC feather, medium dun <40>
Overwing: duck wing primary strip grey; folded over the underwing, 1.5X the body length <19>
Hackle 2: black; 4–5 turns <13>

Comment: If you come across stoneflies in late winter or very early spring, this little guy could be your saviour.

Stonefly Adult, Little Winter Black

Caddisflies

As a searching pattern for creeks and rivers during midsummer after the stonefly and mayfly hatches have dwindled, it's hard to beat a size #12–16 caddisfly to get trout moving and looking up. After hatching, caddisflies will spend several weeks mating, laying several batches of eggs and hanging around their home river, making them available to fish for a much longer period of time than mayflies. Their hatches also overlap, so on a given fishing day, you will likely see different species and a range of sizes and colours presented. In many years while spending time on my favourite river haunts—the Stellako, Crooked and Blackwater rivers of northern BC and the Elk system in the Kootenays—I have fished nothing but caddisflies during a week-long fishing trip.

Caddisfly larvae are available to fish year-round. Pupae are also important and you should have a selection in your fly box, but in moving water, the ascent and transformation to adult happens so quickly an emerger pattern like the CDC Caddisfly is more effective.

The size of your adult caddisflies is important if you wish to fool large trout. A few summers ago on a late August afternoon, while fishing one of my favourite runs on the Stellako, my friend Lloyd Gibson and I fished the hell out of it for a few hours with sizes #14 and 16 CDC Caddisfly Tan, taking a few random 35-cm trout. I felt there should be more fish lying in the run, decided to rest the run for twenty minutes and then make a radical switch to a size #22 CDC Caddisfly of the same colour. Hallelujah! I had one of the highlight fishing days of my life: in one short 10-metre stretch of river, on consecutive casts, eight trout from 40 to 55 cm took the fly and handily let me play them downstream of the honey hole—the fish God can be good!

Caddisfly Larva, Green Rock-worm

Hook: Mustad C53S #14–16
Thread: UTC 70, dark grey
Ribs: white ostrich herl; palmer over the abdomen <17>
Abdomen: dubbing, Stillwater Sparkle, medium olive <37>
Thorax collar: dubbing, Stillwater Sparkle, dark olive <37>
Throat: small, dark grouse feather <8>
Collar: grey ostrich herl; 2–3 turns <10>

Comment: Alternative abdomen/thorax colours are cream/cinnamon or grey/dark olive. This is the larva stage of the Spotted Caddisfly, which does not encase like many other species, but instead builds a net and attaches to the stream bottom, living freely.

Caddisfly Larva, Green Rock-worm

Caddisfly Pupa Emerger

Hook: Mustad C53S #14–16

Thread: UTC 70, dark grey

Tag: 2–3 wraps of orange floss

Ribs: fine gold wire; 5–6 turns over the abdomen <3, 4>

Abdomen: dubbing, Stillwater Sparkle Callibaetis tan <37>

Thorax: dubbing, Stillwater Sparkle dark summer duck <37>

Swimmerets: golden pheasant tippet feather on each side of the body <8>

Collar: 2–3 turns of grey ostrich herl <10>

Comment: Alternative abdomen/thorax colours are grey/medium olive and olive/dark olive.

Caddisfly Pupa Emerger

Caddisfly, Down-wing Tan

Caddisfly Down-wing Tan

Hook: Tiemco 101 #12–16

Thread: UTC 70, tan

Hackle 1: dun saddle; palmer through the body; trim flat over the body <17>

Body: dubbing, Stillwater Soft Blend, Callibaetis tan <37>

Underwing: CDC feather CDC 041, tan <40>

Overwing: pheasant wing primary strip, olive grey; folded over the body and trimmed <19>

Hackle 2: dun saddle; 5–6 turns <13>

Comment: Alternative colours for hackle, body and CDC feather are olive/grey-olive/natural; cinnamon/brown/cinnamon; ginger/yellow/natural; and brown/dark brown/brown. This is one fabulous fly, one of my favourite caddisfly patterns for the Stellako River. I played with this dressing for many years until I added the CDC feather and got it right.

Caddisfly, CDC Emerger Tan

Caddisfly, CDC Emerger Tan

Hook: Tiemco 101 #14–24

Thread: UTC 70, tan

Tail (as shuck): CDC feather natural; body length <40>

Hackle: tan saddle; palmer through the body; trim flat over the body <17>

Body: dubbing, Stillwater Soft Dubbing Callibaetis tan <37>

Wing: deer or elk hairs; body length; trimmed stump at the head <12>

Comment: For small caddisflies, this is the ticket: an Elk Hair Caddisfly with a trailing shuck of CDC. It is my favourite searching pattern for streams in the summer months. I vary the colours of the caddisflies with the CDC feather, body dubbing and wing, matching the hatch in progress. For cinnamon caddisflies, I use tan, cinnamon caddis, and elk hairs; for spotted caddisflies, I use natural, dark hare's ear, and deer hairs.

October Caddisfly

Hook: Mustad R43 #10–12
Thread: UTC 70, hopper yellow
Hackle 1: ginger; palmered through the body; trim flat over the body <17>
Body: dubbing, rabbit/Antron golden brown <37>
Underwing: CDC feather, CDC 041 tan <40>
Overwing: pheasant wing, primary strip, olive grey; folded over the body and trimmed <19>
Hackle 2: ginger; 5–6 turns <13>

Comment: In late summer and early autumn, most streams will offer a sparse hatch of October caddisflies, the largest member of the caddisfly family; trout know what they are and are reckless in their pursuit of them. Alternatively, I'll tie this pattern in hot orange and rusty orange as well, depending on what I observe on the river during my day.

October Caddisfly

Streamers, Baitfish and Minnows

As with still water lakes, smolts and various minnows offer fishes that reside in rivers and streams the best opportunities for high-protein meals, especially during the migration time of early spring, when year-old smolts are venturing to the ocean from their lake nurseries and when young alevin fry are emerging from gravel stream beds. After a long winter surviving in frigid water and perhaps river ice with meagre dining opportunities, fish must be gratified to eat protein and witness the beginning of another year of life in their river.

In river systems, fry are always available to fish. In northern streams, there are pike minnows, Chubb, whitefish, grayling and trout minnows; in coastal habitat, there is a more varied menu of salmon, bullhead, shiner and small ocean species. Streamers are particularly effective for northern rivers that contain bull trout, cannibals of northern mountain waterways that are typically remote and often too sterile to support an abundance of insect life or fish. Bull trout will attack anything that moves and appears edible, but they cannot sustain themselves in rivers that receive heavy angling pressure. You need to go off-track into isolated terrain and waterways to find healthy populations of them.

Streamer and smolt patterns for bull trout, which need to be 6 to 8 cm in length, are best tied on shanks with trailing hooks. This not only increases the length of the fly but also improves the bite and holding capacity of the hook for head-shaking, twisting bulls that at full maturity will commonly reach up to 80 cm in length. Rabbit strip patterns incorporating white, black and red colours combined with some flash and polar bear hairs fish well for them as attractors, and also patterns designed to imitate their favourite prey: northern pike and grayling minnows.

Two of the all-time best general baitfish minnow patterns are the Muddler Minnow, designed by Don Gapen of Anoka, Minnesota, to imitate sculpins, and the Murray's Rolled Muddler, concocted by Tom Murray of Vancouver, BC, a coastal pattern that again imitates general baitfish and sculpins. Both patterns have been around for over fifty years, are timeless in design, and have spawned countless variations.

Another minnow pattern a fly fisher needs for early spring fishing is an imitation that represents the emerging fry of the year, alevins that escape, struggling from their gravel streambed with their egg yolk sacs still intact and not yet absorbed. They look like ghosts, says fisheries biologist and friend John Hagen: small, less than 2 cm in length; pearly silver and white with a little flash; a prominent egg sac under their cheeks; and dominant eyes staring at their new wilderness. I've designed my pattern to mimic these traits.

Rabbit Strip Streamer

Hook: Fish Skull Articulated Shank, 1 3/8"; trailed by Owner #2 bait hook <42>
Thread: UTC 140, white
Tail: rabbit zonker strip, white; length to the end of the trailer hook
Body: pearl Mylar tubing <43>
Flash: 4 strips of pearl Flashabou, doubled; length to the end of the tail <33>
Belly: polar bear hairs; lengths to the end of the tail <46>
Overwing: rabbit strip, white; length to the end of the tail
Cheeks: red ostrich herl; each side of wing
Eyes: painted, black pupil on white <31>

Rabbit Strip Streamer

Grayling Streamer

Hook: Fish Skull Articulated Shank, 1 3/8"; trailed by an Owner #2 bait hook <42>

Thread: UTC 140, white

Body: pearl Mylar tubing <43>

Belly: polar bear hairs; length to the end of the stinger hook <46>

Flash: 2–3 strands of pearl Flashabou on top of the shank, doubled <33>

Overwing 1: sparse polar bear hairs; length to the end of the stinger hook <46>

Overwing 2: sparse polar bear hairs, purple; length to the end of the stinger hook <46>

Overwing 3: Icelandic sheep hairs, olive; extend over all <46>

Eyes: painted, black pupil on yellow <31>

Grayling Streamer

Muddler Minnow

Hook: Mustad S74 #4–6 or R75SNP #10–12
Thread: UTC 140, tan
Tail: oak-coloured turkey strip folded; body length <19, 43>
Ribs: medium gold wire; counter-wrapped over body <3, 4>
Body: gold braid tinsel; coat the ribs and body with flexible cement <43>
Underwing: grey fox tail; body length <46>
Overwing: oak-coloured turkey strips; tail length <19>
Throat: deer hairs <12, 46>
Bullet head: spun deer hairs; clipped to bullet shape <30>

Muddler Minnow

Murray's Rolled Muddler

Hook: Mustad S74 #4–6 or R75SNP #8–12
Thread: UTC 140, red
Tail: mallard feather; body length <8, 9>
Ribs: medium silver wire; counter-wrapped over the body <3, 4>
Body: braided silver tinsel; coat the ribs and body with flexible cement <43>
Wing: mallard feather; apply to end of tail <8, 9>
Bullet head: deer hairs trimmed to expose the red gills' thread underneath <30>

Murray's Rolled Muddler

Alevin Emerger

Hook: Mustad C47SD #6–8

Thread: UTC 140, white

Ribs: medium silver wire; counter-wrapped over the body <3, 4, 43>

Body: pearl Mylar tinsel; coat ribs and body with flexible cement <43>

Belly: polar bear; a few strands 2X the body length <46>

Overwing 1: polar bear; a few strands following the belly <46>

Flash: pearl Angel Hair; 2–3 strands doubled, the length of overwing 1 <33>

Throat: a small section of orange Glo Yarn clipped short; apply a dab of Sally Hansen's when finishing the eyes and apply a finish coat of UV cement

Overwing 2: mallard feather; sparse <8>

Eyes: painted, black pupil on white <31>

Comment: You can vary your emerging fry species with different colours of overwing 2; for example, with olive, brown or black.

Alevin Emerger

Egg Fly

Hook: Mustad 9174 #4–10
Thread: UTC 140, burnt orange
Egg: 2–3 strands of orange Glo Yarn spun on the hook, then pulled and trimmed to shape <44>
Veil: white Glo Yarn <44>

Comment: Alternative Glo Yarn colours are pale pink, bubble gum pink and sockeye red.

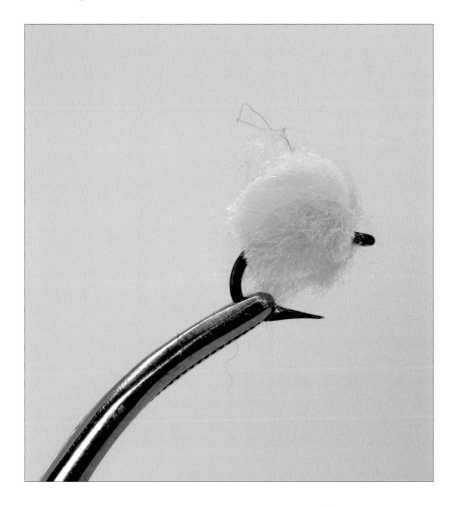

Egg Fly

Terrestrials

In streams and rivers, terrestrials such as ants, beetles, grasshoppers and leaf worms comprise the opportunity scale for fish—they don't go looking for them, but are often on the lookout *for* them. The best days for land and tree bugs to become fish food are warm and windy ones, often in late summer when little else is hatching on the river, and trout are on the prowl for whatever happens to hit the water. Where I live in northern BC, my favourite times to fish these patterns are the lazy, last summer days of September, when mornings are chilly and afternoons are glorious with forest smells, splendid autumn colours and the embrace of a warm sun on my back.

In the still water section, I covered the terrestrial patterns of ants, hoppers and mice. Beetles are another favourite. The one I use is a classic from the vise of innovative US fly tyer A.K. Best called the Winged Bronze Beetle, tied to mimic a struggling beetle that has unwisely lost its bearings and hit the water, its wings spread and fighting to escape the surface film before it becomes a trout's meal. I've altered A.K.'s tie a bit by changing the dubbing colour to sparkle dub and fattening the body, but it's essentially similar.

Winged Bronze Beetle

Hook: Tiemco 101 #16–20
Thread: UTC 70, dark brown
Dubbing ball: dubbing, Stillwater Sparkle, dark summer duck; to divide the wing tips <39>
Wing tips: 2 oval-shaped brown hen hackle tips, tied on each side of the dubbing ball <39>
Shellback: Midge Flex, dark brown
Hackle: brown, stripped on one side; palmer over the body and trim flat top and bottom <6, 17>
Underbody: strand of embroidery thread mid-shank to fatten the body <5, 27>
Body: dubbing, Stillwater Sparkle, dark summer duck <37>

Comment: Alternative colour: all black with dun hackle tips.

Winged Bronze Beetle

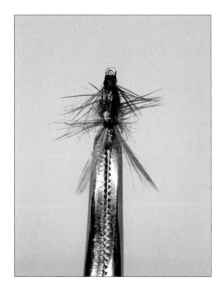

Winged Bronze Beetle

Winged Black Beetle

View from the mountain, Oldman River gap, Alberta. Photo Brian Smith

Photo BJ Smith

Brian Smith is a freelance outdoor writer who has been an accomplished fly tier, rod builder and fly-fishing enthusiast for over fifty years. His specialty is fly-fishing for trout in BC's lakes and streams and the foot-hills' rivers of Southern Alberta, and chasing steelhead and salmon in the watercourses of northwest BC. Smith's work has appeared in *Outdoor Edge* magazine, *Fly Fishing & Tying Journal*, the *Canadian Fly Fisher* magazine and *Northwood Magazine*. He was featured in *Contemporary Fly Patterns of British Columbia*, donated fly patterns to *A Compendium of Canadian Fly Patterns* and was a sponsor and contributor to the publi-cation of a collection of Jack Shaw's diaries, *The Pleasure of His Company*. He was recognized as Contributor of the Year in 1997 for his donations of fly-fishing articles to BC Wildlife Federation's *Outdoor Edge* maga-zine, and in 2008 was awarded the Jack Shaw Fly Tying Award by the BC Federation of Fly Fishers. Smith has previously published *Fly Fish-ing BC's Interior* (Caitlin Press, 2009) and *Seasons of a Fly Fisher* (Caitlin Press, 2013).

Other Books by Brian Smith

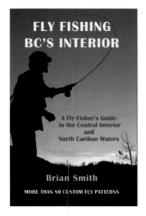

Fly Fishing BC's Interior
A Fly Fisher's Guide to the Central Interior and North Cariboo Waters

978-1-894759-35-9

This is the definitive fly fisher's guide to BC's Central Interior. Brian Smith writes about the allure of BC's wild rainbow trout, which attract fly fishers from all over the world. He describes in extraordinary detail the fabled Blackwater, Stellako and Crooked rivers and the still waters of the Dragon, Hobson, Hart and Wicheeda, renowned trophy lakes that produce rainbow trout weighing up to six kilograms. In this comprehensive guide, Smith shares his award-winning fly tying patterns, his favourite fly techniques and his extensive knowledge of the species, geography, history and fishing lore of the Central Interior and North Cariboo waters. *Fly Fishing BC's Interior* is a must-have, all-inclusive guide for both novice and advanced fly fishers who want to explore in BC's Interior Plateau.

Seasons of a Fly Fisher
Fly Fishing Canada's Western Waters

978-1-927575-05-5

In *Seasons of a Fly Fisher*, Brian Smith takes us on a journey to the Pacific Northwest where we experience the thrill of fishing for salmon and cutthroat trout. He expertly guides us to lakes and rivers in BC's Central Interior that are world-renowned for rainbow trout fishing, then to the Bulkley Valley for steelhead fishing and finally the east Kootenays and southern Alberta for still more trout fishing. *Seasons of a Fly Fisher* is a year-long adventure through the seasons and the harmonies of nature, in which Brian Smith simplifies and demystifies the challenges of this popular sport. Brian's award-winning fly patterns and insightful tips guarantee many years of successful fly fishing.